This book is dedicated to "Miss Elise's" first third grade class,

23 Palestinian children who brought such love and joy to this world and my life.

Elise Sjogren

I want to dedicate this to all the parents who want to see their children

glorify God in greater ways! May this make a big change in your family's life!

Bob Sjogren

i

If you're new to Cat and Dog Theology, you're probably wondering, "What is this all about?"
Cat and Dog Theology helps you see the differences between a God-centered and a people-centered Christianity. Both are found in the church. Its basis is found in a joke about the differences between a Cat and a Dog.

A dog says, "You pet me, you feed me, you shelter me, you love me. **You** must be God."

A cat says, "You pet me, you feed me, you shelter me, you love me, I must be God."

The joke asks a simple question. Do we live for God or does God live for us? Two different answers bring about two totally different Christianities.

Dogs pray to advance God's kingdom. Cats ask God to advance their kingdom.
Dogs seek to make God famous. Cats ask God to make them famous.
Dogs serve God. Cats expect God to serve them.
Dogs ask, "What can I do for God?" Cats ask, "What can God do for me?"
Dogs seek God's face. Cats seek His hand.
Dogs want God. Cats want God's blessings.

These differences can change your entire Christianity. It can change the way you parent your child. It can change the way your child grows up. It can change everything! This book is specifically created to help you in the character development of your children inside your home.

In general, Dogs have great character. Cats do not.

There are three ways you can use these cartoons. Turn the page and find out how!

1. Simply have your children color the cartoon on their own and talk about the different attitudes Cats and Dogs can have using the existing answers and the discussion questions.
2. Hold the cartoon book in your hand and talk about the subject found in the top box. Ask them how they think the Cat would respond and how they think the Dog would respond without letting them see the answer. Then discuss the differences between their answer and the answers given. Who knows, their answer may have been better than the cartoon book's answer itself!
3. Before or after they color it, have them act out both the Dog's attitude and the Cat's attitude. In acting it out, they are much more likely to remember the differences between Cat attitudes and Dog attitudes. Feel free to act it out with them and "ham it up!"

Please note that we all wrestle with Cat Attitudes (we call them "Catitudes") in our lives. This is because we all have an old nature inside of us that has a natural tendency to rebel. Even the Apostle Paul wrestled with it as an adult (see Romans 7:21-23.)

Though we seek perfection (Matthew 5:48), don't expect it from your children. Do expect more Dog attitudes than Cat attitudes as they grow older. When the "Catitudes" do reveal themselves, extend lots of grace to them (along with loving discipline if needed) knowing we all wrestle with Catness inside of us.

Always refer to Cartoon #1 repeatedly. Whether we are a Cat or a Dog, God loves us just the same. We can't earn God's love, this is why His love is unconditional. He loves us simply because He is love——and that's what love does!

Please note that Cat and Dog Theology is also in book form for adults and DVD form for small groups! We also have homeschool curricula created for grades 1-12. See our website for details: www.UnveilinGLORY.com/bookstore.

We pray that this book will help you in training your kids to live out in the world in a way that glorifies God!

How Cats and Dogs respect their babysitter...

When Cats and Dogs are called to dinner...

When It's Time To Get In The Car To Leave...

When Cats and Dogs are told to keep their dresser clean...

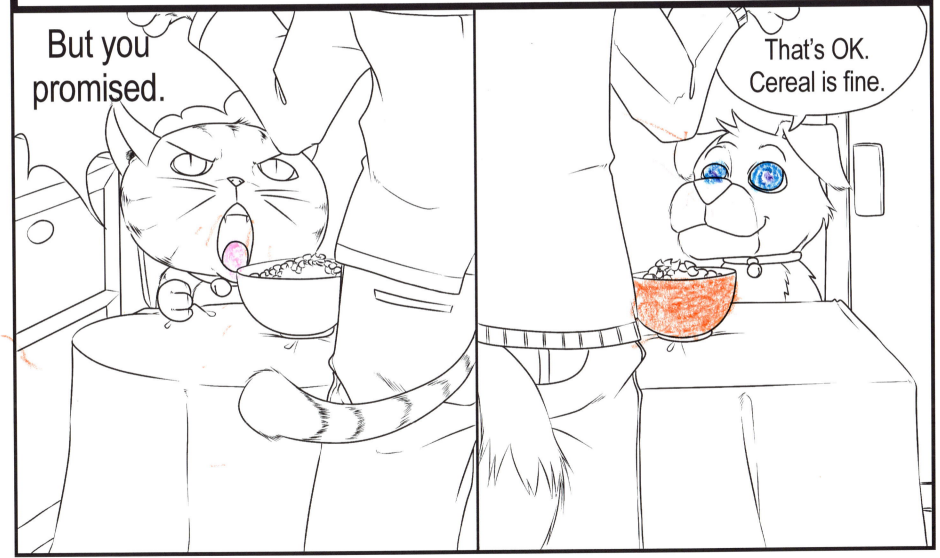

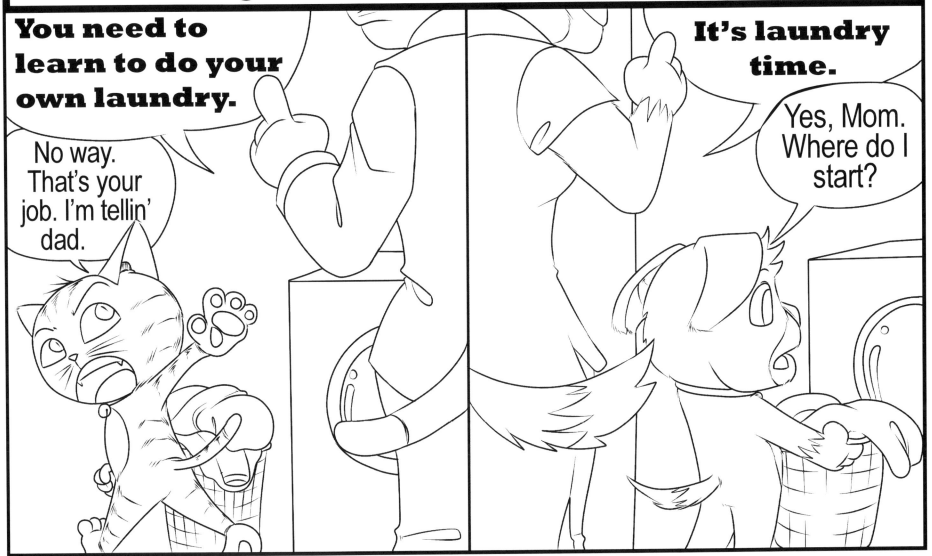

Free time when Mom isn't watching...

We better ask Mom first.

But she'll never know.

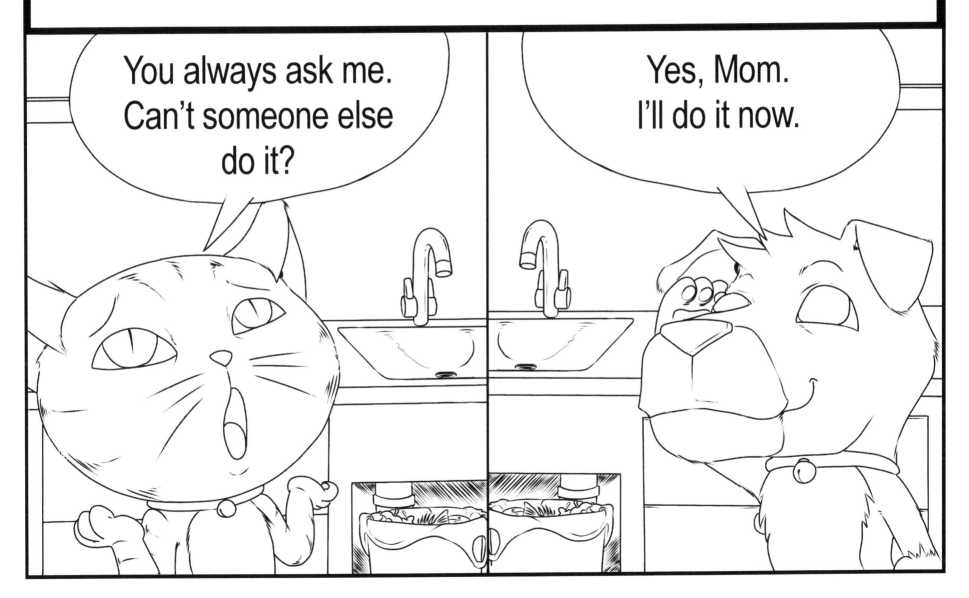

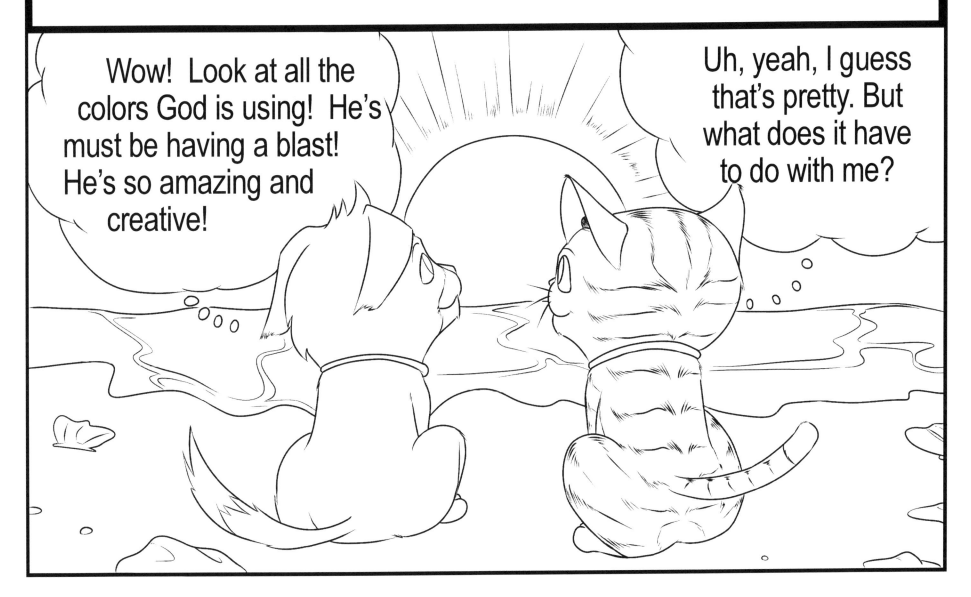

When Cats and Dogs make their bed...

When Cats and Dogs
are asked to put on a coat...

When Cats and Dogs have room time...